Our Air

Nora Treatbaby

Nightboat Books

New York

Nora Treatbaby

ISBN: 978-1-64362-196-8

Design and typesetting by Rissa Hochberger
Typeset in G.B. Jones and Superclarendon

A note on the type:
The display font is based on the title sequence of the 2008 film *The Lollipop Generation* directed by G. B. Jones. Jones is an artist, filmmaker, and musician with a bone to pick. In the early 80s Jones co-founded the post-punk proto-riot grrrl band Fifth Column and in 1985 started publishing the queer punk zine *J.D.s* with co-conspirator Bruce LaBruce out of their rundown apartment in downtown Toronto. The zine's inaugural issue featured the debut of her legendary Tom Girls series. Her drawings continue to be exhibited worldwide. Jones' "no-budget" films often depict the hijinks of bad-mannered girl gangs, homo hustlers, and anarchist mischief-makers. This font was designed by Nat Pyper in 2018 and is the third font in the series *A Queer Year of Love Letters*.

Cataloging-in-publication data is available
from the Library of Congress

Nightboat Books
New York
www.nightboat.org

Contents

nature is a pill
I was made to swallow it.
have I nothing to do with
what's inside of me?
flesh is a full-on commitment
its invitation: a closed circle

if meaning is possible it will
occur on the surface. where is
touching?

I made Earth swallow it
some woman weeps civically
in accordance with her recycling
there is nowhere for any of it to go

what boundaries am I?

a country doth sway
in the long composition
of the map
one fractal preceding
the deepfake of design

I say call off the search
and live in the splendor
of the gerund
self dual
we are to be one
figment repeating yet
at some depth: it wavers, laughs

days filtered through
the screen we use to
resist them. what kind
of loneliness compels us
toward more of it?

leave me be to unsing
the borders of this dream
so I may wander away from
this landscape which I
share with 5G and
the Arby's Stetson hat.

thence a purr
of ancient truth:
this cannot be permanent

a soft wave of silence's
shape
in descension towards
the image of image of

whatiswhatis:
a framework
a curiosity system
a perfect replica of
my butthole

as if we are not free to
pursue thicker things
a life and its span
and measure what is
the duty of the leaf

cuneiform of the torso
when I think of my boobs
I become horny and sad
a creative space

inscribed nothing
and yet exists
my chest it is
a creek bottom
home to a flow
of meanings

similar to the way
light is migratory,
arriving at the moment
of appearance.

they say somewhere
in the city I am hidden
and my task is to find me
all signs point to
other signs

being a woman is
an implausible dream
it is not something you
become / are assigned
it is just an insane vibration

is adequate life coming?
perfect carbless existence in
this museum of breathing
just a tiny piece of substance?
like belief

in exchange of
signals, one thought
follows the sound. cannot
discern the math of
language underneath
intent.

the pronoun is a
sculptural demon
freshly visualized
human sexual value
in each change

in order that we may know sex
sifting it, closing our eyes
to the sound that is
thrashing around
the nipple

observe how logic loves you
good ol' fashioned neutral observation
rendering coeval
with rendering
placed in order to save
life for a later date

skin is not a hug
what really ends?
you?

the world demands
you to imagine it
the situation goes on
and on / it is impossible to
survive duration and yet
acceptance floats into range

there not be a logo for life,
so what of this stuff,
everything yet seen
at one time bought.

and purpose?
the ancient umbel never
faded into some billboard's shade.
we were true,
then and now.

in fact it is all yonder.
I say:
leave the space in space
you cannot rake the forest floor

I will advocate for progress
when I am shown the substance
it's composed of. I know
a straight line can only ever
be empty / from here to there
being everywhere

wind deepens the
hearing world
some rustling
to remind
life of life

I cannot be achieved
I'm not a goal
I say give yourself when
you have yourself
such is
friendship, revolution etc.

love is the porch
upon which I sit
and ponder the
tree its antinoise
which does not
occur

beauty is supposedly
as a drop of dew
a collection of
repeated elements
dissipating into the dome

whence does the rivulet
enjoy the source
of the arching cypress?
who knew 'twould
fuck so?

lush columns of hellfire
& the thinking that governs us
in bare light, in wooded
daylong glint upwardly mobile
in the persistent
movement of structure

each moment there is
no return so we might
need to just accept that.
it is known, the future.

Earth is dropping hints
like "I'm real"
and "love me"

the mystery of freedom
who decided there
was anything but.

lofted into the flash
we are here to do
what with time
broken in all.
unpacked novel
modes of existence
whilst waged

skein of my life
a real thing to waste
dropped from the
near heights of
the conceivable

things are dangled into
the weather / its limits
the world tries to end
but cannot. why?

I need clues, not answers
something inside
a big emptiness
like CVS or sky

it is extremism to have
an economy
society loaded like
some spring
launching into
the end of itself

our aim is not to disperse
things from their categories
but to dissolve the
tenses from which
arrangement is possible

a blossom bloomt
the genius of relation is
tendril between ache
feeling like a desert in one's
own clothes

in spite of cliches
of the multiple
one must ask:
who is not coming
through us?

there is dignity
in flickering like
the passerine song between pines
and being outside of
reality's likelihood.

lost as I am in the specificity
of air, I take breath and it is
a fluency.
I abandon my felicity with language
for the dumb as shit truth
and emit only the clean sound
of sentiment.

light is a river
I am a flume
I am a line that receives heaven
all weather is near
to me always

Seed

so long as the ground survives
these deaf-spots between us
still turn by vibe and by mouth

do rocks cry?

At which depth is further surface, a blossomity towards more light?
Pain is stupid, dude. I need that the feeling of one's own eyes not be
beyond bearable,   and a sprig may hope.

I fled the face of myself
surrendered my present
to a hidden half-world

I wanted smooth pain
that could not be
and to let life linger
on me like a foam

Seed

we cannot tame time
return or take back
what is acted

in what order
do we collapse?   ourselves or another
                          all harm is braided

I eager to clean the pantry
of my distortions,
bathe in real skin
with real people
to see my actions unclothed
with a madness that is
empathy for myself.

and it was in a turning
towards me   what parts of ourselves
                                   we dreamt
                                   severed
                                   I am the sister
                                   of my past selves,
                                   turning towards you

Seed

and what is true
is me
turning
towards

       an assemblage of all
       manner of people
       that I have known
       turning towards
       me associating with
       the seed.

One day we will be hurt in specific ways, like rent. I'm glad my
money's fake. My world began in the trees, behind what was
being written on me.

and there
was us
turning
without no
towardness
                              as if
                              a seed
                              were not
                              in association
                              by the action

Of

Then in so turning

I blurt floras.

There could be

water and light

endless and sieving

one upon the other

in unbroken complexity

why is earth perfect?

I wonder to

what degree has

infinity been verbalized

even my pussy

has a name

turning in a room

with all of you

to slow presentation

down to a crack

or pure mere.

At home in vastness

with the lower leaves

absorbing the

excess of our aspiration.

Earth is not a planet

it is good to live

in a world with sky

my sun is yours.

The common circle

brought us to the

quasi-slaw of

store credit

and sapling syntax

perhaps there is

life's omnivorous

wet which binds

open the seed

turning to

the hilt of some

goose's horn

all distance is

a song through

which no truth

can turn. I have

the witness of

soft titties

but can a person

who gets food

all over themselves

when they eat

really change?

At some middle point

having had nothing

but twinges of

some allogenous fume

I collapsed from

a fathom of my

own abundance in panties

(balls falling out).

I am of so many airports.

Can I just enjoy

the sound of the

dream ending?

Let this be my

expanding mantra:

memory made me weird.

There has been beauty

and now there is

you to receive it

quietly in the edge

of still-sweetness

roaming the echo of

matter. Spent the

morning horny,

such a task these days.

That sports is in the air

is obvious to anyone

struggling to cum.

I still suppose that a

tree can be born

as though not parcel

to some larger

motion of forgetting

and being by

memory and by

mouth a petal cage.

Rather that the turning

of circles was why

a seed billowing

the right grammar

for acoustic fury

to lay down

in the grass

was. Reality is

collaborative but

not consensual.

Door of day opens

with precise roominess

released from sequined

sonar in shirk of

regulation the morning

flows in possible

expansion of

non-distance

by relation to

herbaceous

thicket in semi-splendor

there is no

rectangular time

only groceries.

Colloquial construction

of day being off

or on not dichotomized

by the abundance

of swimmers

or matter charging

in unclenched silkness

but rather by wage

moving through our air

our air frothing with

subjugation and balm.

At least the sky will

finger me, all breasts

being equal on

the backside of

planet lesbian.

I whisper into

mirror dimension:

"don't leave"

& dreamt of walls

a thought unto

my own concavity

a small world unto

a small world

listening for the

evidence involved

with the pleasures

of a vacuum

restored from the

genre of specifics

I vagina like

nobody's watching.

Concerning the trees

we have mentioned

from the beginning

turning, there is a turning

to the top-secret

entrance of the word

which pressed against

the juniper I originate

as a featureless mold

that is engorged

by time here

the sole loci

that time could

enact its stream

and so therefore

turn the circles

toward exactness

and flush certainty

through the self.

Arrival is to have

possessed never

at one time

a single alias

I am wardrobe

malfunctioning

upon infinity's

mattress, twilling

the germane of

humanness with

flotsam of a deeply

personal history

the strands of me

cluster around

the natural knot.

Flowers grow warm

in the clay remembrance

of defunct sexualities.

I would never

use the word "body"

in a poem but

then I saw

AMAB carved into

the bark and

was rerouted to

my sexual god-form.

To be sirening

a petal cage

hovering behind

my technology

I am a fully

realized mass of

oxymoron being so

true to annulment

having sunk so

deeply into beauty.

I was really

fluctuating back there

it's time to explode.

I call for the absolute

redemption of Nora

by breaking through

to the greater

flesh of nothing.

I retreat from

the graph's silent face

these branches are

but furrows

of deeper life

archways between

a reflection scattered

so that one's

proper name

grows dull or real

even now there

is cosmos

in email ink

I left my only

body so that it

would change

I felt the dent

of tenderness

awaken in me

that the sky is blue

and I needn't

complicate this

feeling because

it was never

just a single inquiry

wave after wave

of sexual revolution

only possible

in a world blown

open by waiting

room magazine piles

and the trauma

of parking. There

is a particular echo

to the call of

Who Am I

when yelled

at the exact

moment your city

first gets an

Apple store.

I grew up

desperate to be

born. You can

imagine because

you were there,

awaiting your turn

to ripen in the

freezer aisle,

near Mom, soul

dilating in the

resplendent stucco

of Kroger.

People look amazing

in clothes

in photographs and

that doesn't upset

me anymore.

It is but a lifetime

with leaves spinning

with pleasurable clemency

upon grooves in

the declining tautness

of my face.

As I age

the mirror

grows wiser.

I am turning

towards myself

to write

an apology letter

to Lisa Robertson

for having

pepperoni nipples

and I just say

"Welcome to Love,

my angels."

Where does

the prism go?

To substantiate the

concept of vibrancy

to intern at the flower

to make the stone sexy

it singles us out

against so

many realtors

burning through

the commerce of

surface. My

fingerprint is

a cul-de-sac where

dads spew vibes

vis-à-vis hose length

and Chevy supremacy

light delves

this world

the perfect

for mid-flight tears.

This could be

paradise tomorrow,

same sun turning

us in heaven

as turns this

violent driveway.

So don't term

my touch as

a species of

relation but

as a juniper

swerving recklessly

through definition

in other words

air all air

is fresh you idiots

and we are

not stranded

in proximity to

the soaring twig

alerting form

to the seasons

it is our

same skin

whispering how to

flow outwards

again after

subscribing to Hulu.

I could not

escape that

which was hewn

into the world

during the centuries

I occur

by blaze or

by proxy

we are here.

It can and

will go on

the body of my body.

This old tube.

A feeling of

great rapport

with my AirPods

as it is only

humane to

have distraction.

After everything,

the disheveled past

brings us

toward a blinking

hope of each other

and this is where

I cease turning

but life finds a way

out of the lobby

and into a quiet

existence of ethical

non-monogamy.

gay = good   question mark?

I admit there is

nothing beyond

blue whispers

in the canyon

that just sits.

And a caged fraught.

In the manic

background of

glass flags

we adjourn

sovereignty

as it remains

to be seen

the means to

abolish North America.

Still a fantasy

shakes leafily,

no matter

the forestallment

of turning

to conjoin

our thoughts

and your life.

Pleases the freak

inside the résumé

to unbolt from

a linear history

of the person.

I can no longer

corroborate that

we are touching

except to peel

forth the borders

of our condition

insofar as the

tree was here

I remember her

heaving towards

the sky and

it was relaxing

to imagine ourselves

operating the logic

of juniper branches

as though we could

recollect the

sky, some flirty

twilight that

makes it all touch.

Where does

the fucking time

go? I need

answers.

Whose pocket

and which acre?

I was further

radicalized

by how expensive

it is to sleep.

Turning afield of

the feeling of feeling

alright, I am lost.

Existence is distant.

How normal to have

found myself

shattered during

beltway transhumance.

I am a lady

but you can

call me dude.

I cannot

recall the experience

of womanhood

prior to it

overtaking me.

Perhaps there

is a missing memory,

some spring in

dappled forest

sending forth pink

spumes through

vaginal rock walls,

molten chromosomes

hardening into the

bright stone of

a labial pool.

Perhaps I drank

this delicious

froth, sundering me

from a destiny

of exactly what I

cannot say. So is

life as a lady

deemed to be despite

serious objections

to the paradigm.

She works

the morning light

between uncertain

gaps in the self

having proceded

in the task

of establishing

a set of axioms

to throw directly

into the trash.

I am a riverbank

as such I wash away.

I will live free.

I will be perceived.

I am a softening spray of love.

Just like love, I suck.

I will hem

the elusive strokes

of our image

into some reverie

that solves us.

I will get distracted.

In the pure engine

of your twenties,

one is stopped short

of exactness.

Is being trans

important? I lose

my surroundings

what is near

so vast and

I so small.

The supernumerary

of cranes dot

our clouds,

our sky,

our heaven and

we are left

bloodthirsty

for a view

of the end

each day I gaze

on my friends

cute butties

and kneel in the dumb

truth of optimism.

A body is just

replacement space

for the limitless truth

of each other

but also where

the centuries

actually occur

history has a form

in bruise

it is not just

eye contact.

Did I not

say "hope"

back there

in the trees

awash in some

sudden humor

of our situation

which is changing

like a stone

did I not say

"let's pretend

we possess time

of a different

aura so to

suck the

chlorophyll of

the juniper to spin

ourselves a flotational

shape to escape

our heaving in

this warm

ecstasy of being

a creature

that moves

just like a stone

turning to the

grammar that

speaks open the

decline of touch."

Suck the perfect

apprehension

from the landscape.

Vibe check on surface.

Ample Family Dollars

on mute highways

receding into

prefigurative vegetation

and powerlines

interlocked with

incalculability. The old

neighborhood is afflicted

with latte madness.

Miniature urban suburb.

Nominal Tyvek tsunami

to thwart Google

Maps refugees.

Discharge millennia

of psychosexual planning

through question of

what to wear

at work. We are

penalized for

both sides of

perception. If

I am to be alleged

as having some

hot blood I will

have it be known

I spew face

down the same

laughter as the

bushes behind

the Wawa.

Ok love, what do

you want from us?

Large and light and

completely receptive to

the myth of

underlying myth

and what do we get?

A lifetime's supply

of perfection.

Turning towards

a deep romance

of possibility.

Having only ever

been given

no choice.

There are worlds.

Tree

juniper baby
you swell, churn and fill
like a meat in the mouth

it is not taste   it is not sight it is not the wayfaring twig

that binds wind and cracks
open that nothing from
which you are free.

juniper baby
there is lucky air crisping
around your branch
inside of you profuse
movement
archaic and warped

could it be a sexless pleasure?

stillness united with torsion and throb
spoken by sparse tunneling of russet-tongue
we are lovers
I love you

Tree

the tree isn't
is it not
plain to see
in so-called "West"

pure stagger between
sustaining and
ripening

                        ripening
                        a pleasure so collapsing
                        movement along nothing

what budding what woodedness is permitted in philosophy
reconciled with value of that which is mere spaciousness? Such
that things are their intervals, such that the thinking of things is
their beauty / their expiration.

                        in future languages of
                        the stem
                        I never thought
                        this thought

Juniper is a thought. Thriving upon the backends. The plant, it is a tree. She/he has internalized life, all beauty arranged outward from a nonchalance. The skin of its bark stretched through the hoop of time's salvage. Balloon-shaped heartbreak is emanating from Juniper. A blank describes it while another blank utilizes it while another blank invents it. Juniper says nostalgia for mass-produced objects refound in thrift stores is the same feeling as being destituted by life on Earth's collapse. It is about questioning our attachments. Juniper is found object, variance a feature of mass-produced landscape. Ansel Adams' invisible hand moves a world into index. Pure juniper in the out of bounds. We are walking around a desert of our own motives. One single juniper twisting in its bark towards a hatched blue sky. I can see long lines of clouds going backwards. Conceived wind, its path imagined. Juniper is snatched from the continuous world by the crane of definement. Juniper is wave after wave of representation. But juniper has terms its image cannot pronounce, gathering itself again.

Tree

this or that beauty. how is one to distinguish?

I, opening.   tree unfolding tree.

recall prayer, how our legacy is of tying it to a post in the desert
and abandoning it.

>O flag
>so stupid
>a gash in the
>sky falling
>forever

leaves,   light,
nothing's separate
the world is its atmosphere, also

a small gap of scorched earth between two types of living

what is between life what
is between time what moves?
  clouds move by breezes you cannot feel

Tree

cannot trust what is made
or comes from a making process
knowledge therefore banished

a dream believed weird to touch
don't forget
truth is a window
only ever partial

and when we came to a spatial space
it was lines and hues set against
words and their policies.
one could act an anchor to the world like "weird
and another just a diversion, like "woman."

a word
is unlivable
just go out
and scream
the crisis
in each
sound
be gay

Love

A flaw. Could there be conceived a more superior opening? An injury to the outwardness of things / a leak in time's little shell. We are witness not so much to ourselves as to each other, and so we appear in the emotional history of perception. So flush with strata. Awash in taxa. Species defined at the end of its variation. The induvial is but a small remainder. We are given the clean slate of a perfect silhouette. Reality being primordial, we undergo it. Thrown universe, slightly adrift of the outline. Spilt from a thong. An ear turned inwards toward the gravitational law of thine own genitals. What disturbs the placid waters of the celestial dish? Politics and the gist of it. Ideas abound and I am divided. The sky is like a melted swatch expanding like the universe towards imperceptible constructions. Perfect for conversation. I recounted my day at work and sort of just whimpered a dying rose into my ice water. We sketched a cosmogony of depth. Found none. Is time a delay? We devise each other in exchanges of that nature although at this conjuncture all the world's a contract. The self is its continually deferred penalty. Metaphysics builds a house but not a home. Nonetheless you've fashioned the boards and planks of my ass into a bed for your hand. How does one move as if foliage? Quivering in rebellion against those that reason duplicating beauty could be anything but a distrust in what is near to the source of what is. This photography of the wind zips us into skin from the organized ocean. My eyes are sewn into this version of seeing. Each to each, till we are all just eaching. For want of perfect explanation, and so it is we are dominated. Identity rents us to each other. And yet for flaw, there is nowhere to appear. The world is complete and unlimited. Unlimited renewal, complete opening. One penis snapping in the wind flagging naught.

Passage

profits grow but cannot flower
coarse road of soil
cuts away from the range
frees itself underneath
the surface
of the "plot."
I am still small compared to
what water perceives, and so
this is the sense in which I
strive to become deep.
quoting a rock in the ground:
"abolish chronology"

words without synonyms
water and time
capital cannot understand
language aches to be used
each unit a dump truck
of significance. it is
spoken by touch and taste
no data can break the surface
of our skin of our masturbation
what we need what we use
to repeat to replenish
our descriptions.

when thought of time as it is a verb
establishing distinct parameters
in abstract movement deferred
time, in essence, an
event making action
seconds between years between eras
waiting
for the necessary violence
freedom deferred
when thought of time reaches its extreme
necessary perforations in history
no limits to what can be called time

it is our life's work to struggle
against something so useless as profit.
land becomes impregnated
with systems of use
instead of just use. what
can be borne of these seasons,
planned as they are to repeat?
life such as ours split into a metronome
simplicity is sealed from us
commander of Project Human
now that the world is real
science is nearly complete

under unnamed optimism
if I sense my life it is always
distinct from that which sustains it
jobs prove nothing
there is no image between us
that is exactly like money
it occurs that there are
fumes persisting from
an earlier floral situation
if upon an angle in your face
there was timber, they
would cut you down as well.

Hello, Earth

I aspire to behave as if a beach, shaped in the
supreme sequence of orbit, a line that imbibes
grace, the end and possibility of all green motion,
totally pointless, elliptical fade, a place to rest that
falls freely, grainy footage, a receding border,
underneath the masturbating star, pearl caked, a
tempo vision, wink of the universe.

I aspire to behave as if a pond, tiny and clear,
home to a few, one of many flecked throughout
some larger assembly, humble sustenance for
those who would be my neighbor, a damp hole,
an earth sequin, dug in deep, liquid at peace,
whirling beyond sight, a marbled mirror of
my own environment, existing without noise,
sexually rippling sexlessly.

After the waterfall we were eating. We
learned that all varietals of the common
bean are native to the Americas, and you
cried. I feel humbled by the transit of
plants you said. I cried. I gave a guy a ride.
It was raining. On the phone, I said I wish
I'd never hurt anyone. You said sometimes
all a person may need is a ride to Burger
King. I cannot resound the orchestration of
that day without admitting some things. I
wish I'd never been born. I wish I had been
born a bean. You said it is vulnerable to be
in awe. You said the vibrations of kinship
w a stranger can change you. You said
touched by the experience, physically.

After the waterfall, we were eating. We
learned that all varietals of the common
bean were native to the Americas, and you
cried. I feel humbled by vegetables you
said. I cried. I gave a guy a ride. It was
falling, light and rain from the same sky.
On the phone, I said I am surrounded by
distances. You said I only know confused
people. I cannot resound the orchestration
of that day without admitting some things.
I wish the truth was real. I wish I had been
born a bean. I said we exist for each other.
You said it is vulnerable to be in awe. You
said the vibrations of kinship w a stranger
can change you. You said touched by the
experience, physically.

After the waterfall, we were eating. Later,
we would hear angels, screaming. I feel
humbled by the transit of plants, you said.
I cried. I performed the transit of plants,
my seed to where another's shore opened.
It was raining. On the phone I said I wish
I'd never hurt anyone. You said sometimes
it is possible to outlive your outline. I
cannot resound the orchestration of that
day without admitting some things. You
are the world moving through me. I feel
moved by the tenderness of complexity.
You said it is vulnerable to be in awe. You
said the vibrations of kinship w a stranger
can change you, you said to let the world
penetrate our speaking.

After the waterfall, we were eating. We
learned that all varietals of the common
bean are native to the Americas, and
you cried. I feel humbled by the transit
of plants you said. It was raining. I gave
a guy a ride. On the phone, I said in the
world, I am real. You said sometimes all
a person may need is distance. I cannot
resound the orchestration of that day
without admitting some things. I feel like I
failed as a human being. I wish I had been
born a bean. You said it will be possible
to retrieve beauty. You said the vibrations
of kinship w yourself can change you. To
wait.

At the waterfall, we were vibing. Its
propulsions were of rain from days ago.
Time was soft and the movement peaceful.
We flowed downstream, together. I feel
humbled by vegetables you said. I cried.
I gave a guy a ride. It was normal. I said
there are moments in each day that clarify
our alignments. You said sometimes all a
person may need is to give a guy a ride
to Burger King. I cannot resound the
orchestration of that day without admitting
some things. Every narrative is pliable to
truth, eventually. You said what we do is
just the world moving through us. I said I
just want there to be room in the world for
me. You said it is vulnerable to be in awe.

After the waterfall, we exit ourselves and
join the world. And so the mechanics of
redemption did not feature gravity. One
casts a limitless spell. That is life. I did
not go inside myself to observe what I
am but rather what I touch. You said to
pose as a bean, you will need light, rain.
I cannot resound the orchestration of
distance without everything crying. I wish
had never been born. I wish I had born
a bean. You said we are each other, but
that it is concealed from us. You said it is
vulnerable to be in awe, you said that we
are each other.

After the waterfall, we were eating. We
cried. I feel humbled by the transit of
plants you said. That summer I had joys in
my heart. I saw mushrooms bathing. I saw
two weird people hug. It did not redeem
me, but it filled us all. On the phone, I
heard angels, screaming. I don't know
anyone who isn't confused on how to fill
themself. You said sometimes all a person
may need is distance. I cannot resound the
orchestration of that day without admitting
some things. The distance felt like a
violence. At the end of all the violence lies
a bean. You said it is vulnerable to be in
awe. You said the world will change as you
do, you said this is our air.

Put aside the question of yourself and touch
something. I feel I must do housekeeping in
a room that is only love so that there may
be a retrograde in our politics towards that
door, it is yellow and it is distance, it is a
portal to greater awe and it never closes.
The touching exchange was a profound
entrance to something more vast than
accountability, how we transact pain. I was
interwoven with all pain as I had touched
it, touching me, and it was love. Nothing
was rare in that moment. I had given a guy
a ride. It is normal to wish to be gentle and
to fail. No one gets dispensation from the
vibration of violence, either side of it. The
world will suffer no ratio. It is here and
now, whole in all of us. We move through
each other, endlessly. Later, there are
angels, screaming. The world will suffer no
ratio. There was beauty. I don't know why.
The sky. I can see it beneath me. Rain and
light before and after me. Here, we are real.
There were mushrooms bathing. There
is nothing left to be said of our outlines,
so you said I feel humbled by the transit
of plants. I thought deeply of our limits
and witnessed a choreography between
us of distance and pain but the movement
was you being the world moving through
me moving through you and it wasn't a
language of harm in the orchestration of
that day. It is not strange what there is not

a word for. To place things in their cosmic situation is to know exactly what a friend is. I saw two weird people hug. Everything I have done has been so love can come home to me. This is the drama of becoming. We are each other, endlessly. I cannot resound the orchestration of that day without admitting some things. Truth is an energy. Unfortunately, it is my teacher, I am alive so I am violent and I am real so it was raining. On the phone I admitted I had hurt people. I did not know I was real, or here. Despite the rain, despite the collaboration of the bean and touch, distance and Burger King, two weird people hugging, all invested by one braid of violence and love following from truth. Love made Nora. We were there. It was earth. We were eating. We learned that all varietals of the common bean are native to the Americas. You cried. You said I feel humbled by the transit of plants. I cried. The world was moving through me as you. It was raining, light. You said it will come home to you. I cannot resound the orchestration of that day without admitting some things. I can only say what a friend is. I can only say simple things. All the words for new are old. You said I only know confused people. You said everything we do is so love can come home to us. You said touched by the experience physically.

After the waterfall we were eating.
We learned that everything occurring
is a portal to greater awe, and you cried.
I feel humbled by vegetables, you said. I
cried. I gave a guy a ride. It was raining.
On the phone, I said I just want there to
be room in the world for me. You said our
days are not numbered, they exist, for us.
We are continuous w angels, screaming.
I cannot resound the orchestration of that
day without admitting some things. You
said welcome to love, my angels. You said
distance does not need to be a language of
pain. You said here, we are real.

After the waterfall we were eating. We
learned that all varietals of the common
bean are native to the Americas, and you
cried. I feel humbled by the transit of
plants you said. I cried. I gave a guy a ride.
It was raining. On the phone I said I wish
I'd never hurt anyone. You said sometime
all a person may need is a ride to Burger
King. I cannot resound the orchestration
of that day without admitting some things.
All harm is braided. My air is yours. You
said it is vulnerable to be in awe. You said
the vibrations of kinship w a stranger
can change you, you said touched by the
experience, physically.

Leaving

We endeavored to think of something we love whether infinite only, or on the surface of the world precisely so that we know acts of recognition exist and one could then have a thought like this: *I am like you* to which I said I wish I had never hurt anyone and now the world is being remade in the image of regret but the feeling is falling away. The means of relation available to us seeks the privation of time a shared resource we have no

choice but to surrender eventually and maybe my other body
is free to give it away by breathing but here in this world
we have to fight to live the way we could because capitals
communication between disparates is not yet an interval but
the present moment is always sparkling w our prayer to be
collected in flux screaming *this is our time* and thus overthrow
this loneliness, the gap between all things and say to each other
we are each other.

ACKNOWLEDGMENTS

Thanks to *Bæst: a journal of queer forms and affects,* e-flux, and *The Recluse,* where some of these poems appeared previously, and to Other Weapons Distro for putting out *Hope Is Weird,* the chapbook that was the jumping-off point. Thank you to Lindsey Boldt, Santi Valencia, Gia Gonzales, and Nightboat Books for making the book a reality, which is really a dream, and special gratitude to Rissa Hochberger because it is a good life in which I get to share the making of this book with my sister. Thank you to everyone at the Bard MFA program for giving such focus to my work. It was a hot beam of thought that made me a better artist, probably a better person. Love and love to all the friends, teachers, and collaborators whose insights and support directly touched the shape of my book, especially but not absolutely limited to Ted Rees (and everyone in the Overflowing workshops, far too many to name), Carolyn Ferrucci, Kaur Alia Ahmed, Hilary Johnson, Saralee Stafford, Irene Silt, Pam Lins, Rosie Stockton, Drew Zeiba, Laura Huertas Millán, Oliver Silverman, Greg Nissan, and Christopher Rey Pérez.

These poems started out as probings of my despair. Why was our world inhospitable to our lives? The surface of the Earth returned to me daily, redeeming everything I had come to understand as loss. The juniper shone a shape that gave my body permission to be nothing for a while. I lost a lot of friends but I gained even more. Light shone on my shape and I decided to change it. Earth declined, love occurred, hope sprang, vibes continueth. To my friends who sustained me during this time, I learned so much about living that now

I call it forgiveness. Nelle, Ricky, Honey, Emir, September, Lyra, Tommy, Matia, Dylan, Alex, Jean, Halo, Willa, Marge, Allie, and Zoey. Names inadequate to the inseparable web that produces me, produces this. A deeply loving sound of gratitude—something I cannot make but might be recalled by the incandescent song of water at High Falls—to MJ Hicks who said so much so that I could say all this.

NORA TREATBABY is a writer and artist based in New York State. *Our Air* is her first book. She has published two previous chapbooks, *I <3 2 Swim* (2022) and *Hope Is Weird* (2020). She does not spend her time.

NIGHTBOAT BOOKS

Nightboat Books, a nonprofit organization, seeks to develop audiences
for writers whose work resists convention and transcends boundaries.
We publish books rich with poignancy, intelligence, and risk. Please
visit nightboat.org to learn about our titles and how you can support our
future publications.

The following individuals have supported the publication of this book.
We thank them for their generosity and commitment to the mission of
Nightboat Books:

Kazim Ali
Anonymous (8)
Mary Armantrout
Jean C. Ballantyne
Thomas Ballantyne
Bill Bruns
John Cappetta
V. Shannon Clyne
Ulla Dydo Charitable Fund
Photios Giovanis
Amanda Greenberger
Vandana Khanna
Isaac Klausner
Shari Leinwand
Anne Marie Macari

Elizabeth Madans
Martha Melvoin
Caren Motika
Elizabeth Motika
The Leslie Scalapino - O Books Fund
Robin Shanus
Thomas Shardlow
Rebecca Shea
Ira Silverberg
Benjamin Taylor
David Wall
Jerrie Whitfield & Richard Motika
Arden Wohl
Issam Zineh

This book is made possible, in part, by grants from the New York City
Department of Cultural Affairs in partnership with the City Council and
the New York State Council on the Arts Literature Program.